DANIEL AND THE LIONS

This story has been extracted from
Read Aloud Bible Stories, Vol. 3
by Ella Lindvall

Printed in Mexico

MOODY PRESS

Daniel was the king's helper.
Daniel was the king's friend.
Daniel was God's friend, too.
He talked to God every day.

One day the king said, "EVERYBODY STOP PRAYING! You must pray just to ME! If you pray to God, I'll put you where the lions are!"

Now Daniel heard
what the king said.
Daniel thought
about the lions.
Daniel said,
"I will pray to God anyway."
So—

Daniel went home.
He went upstairs.
He got down on his knees.
And he talked to God.

The next day
Daniel talked to God again.
Soon the king's men came.
They saw Daniel praying,
and they ran to tell the king.

They said, "Daniel is talking to his God!"
"Oh, my," said the king.
He didn't want to put Daniel where the lions were.

"Oh, my," said the king.
He was sad.
He liked Daniel.
But at last he said,
"Daniel, your God
will take care of you."

So they put Daniel
down, down, down
into the lion place.
Then everybody
went home.

The lions saw Daniel.
The lions heard Daniel.
The lions smelled Daniel.
But the lions didn't bite Daniel.
Do you know why?

Because GOD SHUT THEIR MOUTHS!

In the morning
the king came running.
"Oh, Daniel!" he said.
"Was your God strong enough?
Could He save you
from the lions?"

And Daniel said, "YES, O king! My God sent His angel to shut the lions' mouths. They haven't hurt me at all."

Now the king
was VERY happy.
He said to his men,
"Pull Daniel up
out of the lion place!"

So they pulled Daniel
up, up, up,
out of the lion place.
They looked at his face.
They looked at his hands.
They looked at his feet.
The lions hadn't even
scratched him.

What did you learn?

God was strong enough
to take care of Daniel.
God is stronger than lions.
God is strong enough
to take care of you.

About the Author

Ella K. Lindvall (A.B., Taylor University; Wheaton College; Northern Illinois University) is a mother and former elementary school teacher. She is the author of *The Bible Illustrated for Little Children,* and *Read-Aloud Bible Stories, volumes I, II, and III.*